The Potential For Russian Exploitation of the Saami Indigenous Peoples of Finland

Samuel Ryu

ISBN-10: 1727443756
ISBN-13: 978-1727443752

CONTENTS

1 KEY FINDINGS

- Finland's minority and indigenous people, the Saami, have been marginalized and violated by the Finnish government on numerous occasions. Finnish Saami stand at odds with the Finnish government due to increasing industrialization and militarization in northern Finland, where the Finnish Saami reside.

- Rifts between Finnish Saami and the Finnish government may present themselves as exploitative opportunities for the Russian regime. These rifts may be exploited to serve Russia's Arctic interests by preventing or delaying Western industrialization and militarization close to the Arctic and the Kola peninsula.

- The Finnish government has plans for inoculating Finnish civil society against influence operations. While confidence exists for general Finnish psychological resilience, Finland is largely homogenous, and an "out" group, such as the Saami, has existing resentment against the Finnish government itself, which may be exacerbated through increased perceptions of alienation, exploitation, and oppression by the Finnish government. The Finnish Saami may be at a critical point, as even reconciliation attempts by the Finnish government have been met with anger and suspicion.

- Russia has emplaced individuals with government links into oversight positions within Saami political groups in Russia. Russia has historically viewed and contemporarily views the Saami as an intelligence threat due to the Saami's trans-national networks which extend across the Nordic states and into Russia's Kola peninsula.

- The Russian government's infiltrative control over the Russian Saami reflects the regime's agenda to superficially preserve the Saami while prospecting for natural resources in the Arctic region, expand its military reach, and control the Russian Saami's political ambitions.

- It is possible that Russia's infiltrative control over the Russian Saami may also serve a counter intelligence function. However, due to Russian governmental involvement in trans-national Saami groups as well, it is also possible that such control may serve as an intelligence function against the West.

2 INTRODUCTION

The Finnish Saami are a disenfranchised and distinct minority group in northern Finland that may be vulnerable to indirect Russian influence operations. The Saami indigenous peoples are distributed across the northern areas of Norway, Sweden, Finland, and Russia. Due to Russia's economic and military activities in the Arctic regions and the Kola peninsula, northern Finland may become increasingly important for economic and military purposes. However, industrialization and militarization of northern Finland causes rifts with the Finnish Saami.

It is possible that Russia may utilize the Russian Saami (Kola Saami) against the Nordic Saami by controlling its narratives, misrepresenting its relationship with Russia, and highlighting the repression faced by the Nordic Saami. The Kola Saami's political groups are presided over by Russian state-linked individuals who do not genuinely represent Saami political interests. Such infiltrative control may serve Russian counter intelligence and intelligence purposes against the West, as the Saami have been perceived as foreign intelligence threats by the Russian government.

Russian influence operations against the Finnish Saami will likely seek to prevent or delay Finnish industrialization and militarization of its northern area. Through humanitarian narratives, existing Saami grievances may be amplified and weaponized against the Finnish government. Exploiting cultural rifts is a known hybrid warfare tactic. Continued Finnish governmental marginalization and political repression of the Saami will likely cause more resentment and increase the potential for exploitation by external actors.

3 BACKGROUND

Finland's *Security Strategy for Society*[i] seeks a whole-of-government approach towards internal defense that incorporates civil society. This strategy includes inculcating psychological resilience against influence operations, and is likely a lesson learned from studying Russia's influence operations against Ukraine.[ii] While such pre-emptive protections may benefit Finnish society at large, minority groups may have been overlooked. The Finnish Saami is a minority group, and is the smallest minority (0.1%) within an ethnically Finnish country that is largely homogenous (93.4%).[iii]

The Finnish Saami are not truly integrated into Finnish society, and possess cultural self-governance rights under Finland's 1999 Constitution. While indigenous rights and interests are listed as a part of Finland's *Action Plan for the Update of the Arctic Strategy*,[iv] Finland has not ratified the *International Labor Organization Convention No. 169* to protect indigenous peoples,[v] and the Saami have numerous complaints against the Finnish government.[vi]

While violating the Finnish Saami may not have been the intention of the Finnish government, it is very possible that those actions have been accelerated by Russia's increased military presence in the Arctic regions. The Finnish Saami primarily reside in northern Finland, where Finland only has one air force base and some army units. Most of Finland's military is concentrated along its southern and south-eastern borders. In contrast, Russia has a concentration of nuclear weapons on the Kola peninsula, in addition to maintaining a military presence along its borders with the Baltic states.

The Saami are dispersed across the Nordic states and extend into Russian territory on the Kola peninsula. Due to the Kola peninsula's military importance, activities near it are heavily scrutinized. Tensions between Russia and the West provide pretext for heightened sensitivity in the area. In this type of environment, the Saami find themselves in a precarious position, as they are viewed with suspicion by Russia for having networks that extend across the Nordic states.

While Russia's concerns about the Saami have primarily stemmed from political and security interests, the history of the Saami in Nordic states show perceived colonialism and race-based tensions as pre-existing conditions prior to being exacerbated by the current geopolitical climate. Comparatively, the Russian Saami receive the best superficial treatment. However, the Russian Saami are different due to Russian governmental infiltration into Russian Saami political groups. While the Saami possess divided views about their respective states of residence, Finland's violation of existing protections for indigenous groups have made it conspicuously anti-Saami.

Russia has previously demonstrated influence operations techniques against Finland's Russian population, e.g. portraying Finland as a child-kidnapper that separates mixed Finnish-Russian families.[vii] Other concerning developments include the presence of Finnish pro-Kremlin academic, Johan Backman, as a current candidate for Lapland's parliament through the umbrella political group Reformi,[viii] Backman was linked to the Russian Institute for Strategic Studies, a Russian think tank linked to the Kremlin,[ix] and has also supported MV-lehti, an independent, Finnish news organization that opposes Finnish involvement with N.A.T.O and the European Union.[x] In 2017, Backman organized a political event to accommodate Aleksandr Dugin as the guest speaker in Helsinki.[xixii] Backman's ascension to Lapland politics will likely serve Kremlin interests by opposing Western militarization in northern Finland.

Whlle Backman's narrative is tailored to Finnish Russians, most Finnish Russians are dispersed in south and southeastern Finland.[xiii] However, northern Finland in the Lapland area does contain Russian speaking inhabitants, and is only lesser in comparison to higher concentrations of Russian speakers in south and southeastern Finland.[xiv] The Saami languages belong to the Uralic language family, but most of the Russian Saami on the Kola peninsula have adopted Russian. The loss of language is an indicator that is consistent with the Russian Saami's lack of political self-determination and an increasingly diluted culture that is being appropriated by the Russian government. Control of the Russian Saami by the Russian government, combined with potential political subversion in Lapland by pro-Kremlin activists such as Backman, may create optimal conditions for Russian political influence operations against Finland's Arctic policies.

4 ANALYSIS

The Finnish Saami continue to perceive oppression by the Finnish government. Logging expansions[15] and railway construction plans[16] by the Finnish government may disrupt Saami food sources and alienate the Saami from their historical lands. Existing protections for the Finnish Saami are sparse or non-existent, especially regarding food and land rights.[17]

At the heart of the issue, the Saami are angry at the failure of the Finnish government to inform the Saami of changes to legal protections that the Saami rely on, the failure to consult with the Saami prior to governmental activities in Saami areas, and the failure to pass legislation to give the Saami more concrete legal protections. In 2017, reconciliation attempts by the Finnish government were viewed suspiciously by the Saami.[18]

The Finnish Saami may be co-opted or supported by trans-national or international groups which seek to halt Western militarization. Outside of political recourse, the Finnish Saami have engaged in physical protests. In 2017, Saami activists camped on government lands to protest perceived violations of indigenous fishing rights.[19] More recently, Greenpeace Canada and Cree Nation joined the Finnish Saami to protest the Finnish government's railway construction plans, which cuts through lands that the Saami rely on.[20] Given the marginalized political status of the Finnish Saami, long-standing grievances against the Finnish government, and the shared goals of other organizations in preventing Western militarization, it is possible that the Finnish Saami may actively seek political support and exposure through external organizations.

Finland's increasing militarization is likely caused by Russian military build-up in the Arctic and the Kola peninsula. In 2015, Finland established quick reaction forces to be utilized in offensive roles, and deployed them along its border with Russia.[21] Finland also stated the necessity for legislative reformation to ensure greater military readiness.[22] Qualitative improvements and quantitative increases to Finland's military, in cooperation with Nordic and N.A.T.O states,[23] is an indicator into Finland's threat assessment of Russia. In Lapland, Finnish special operations forces have been training for combat operations in Arctic climate, indicating preparation for potential combat operations in the north.[24] Increases in such training exercises would further signal the attention being given to northern Finland.

Despite the lack of heavy military presence in northern Finland, it is likely that Russia views the northern Lapland region with heightened suspicion. N.S.A-Norway intelligence activities against "Russian targets in the Kola peninsula" and Russian civilians related to Russia's energy policy,[25] further confirmed by admitted espionage activities in Kirkenes on behalf of Norwegian intelligence,[2627] only serves to reinforce Russia's perceptions against the West. Russia's nuclear forces on the Kola peninsula and the area's strategic value due to its transportation routes are legitimate concerns. Compounding these concerns is the presence of the Saami on the Kola peninsula.

Russia views the Saami as a foreign intelligence threat due to its trans-national presence in the Nordic States and the Kola peninsula. Saami activists have been labeled as foreign agents by Russia.[28] However, treatment of the Saami as foreign agents may be seen in Soviet history as well. The Saami were viewed by the Soviet Union's NKVD as foreign intelligence operatives due to the Saami's trans-national presence. These concerns led the NKVD to murder a few dozen Saami in the 1930s, accusing them of spying for Finland and attempting to create an independent Saami republic.[29] While Finland is not a N.A.T.O member, its non-aligned status does not preclude it from cooperating with N.A.T.O members.

To combat its perceived threat from the Saami and the West, Russia may be employing counter intelligence measures against the Saami by controlling it with state-linked individuals through the pretense of caring for the Saami. Russia's concerns for indigenous people's welfare is superficial. Despite mentioning indigenous peoples' welfare in its Arctic policy,[30] Russia's actions show contradictions. Saami organizations relevant to Russia, the Association of the Kola Saami (A.K.S) and the Russian Association of Indigenous Peoples of the North (R.A.I.P.O.N), are both led by state-linked individuals who have come to power through state interference and corruption.

The interests of the Russian Saami on the Kola peninsula are not genuinely represented by the current leaders of A.K.S and R.A.I.P.O.N. Elena Goy, the current president of the A.K.S., came to power through questionable processes.[31] Goy is linked to the Murmansk Regional Center of Indigenous Peoples of the North,[32] which is subordinate to the Murmansk Regional Government. Murmansk's Minister of Domestic Policy and Mass Communications, Gleb Shinkarchuk,[33] met with Goy after her election as president of the Association of the Kola Saami.[34] In contrast, Valentina Sovkina, a pro-Saami activist who won the Kola Saami presidency in 2014,[35] was illegitimated by the Russian government and intimidated.[36]

R.A.I.P.O.N's current president, Grigory Ledkov, is also head of Russia's Permanent Delegation of the State Duma to the Nordic Council. R.A.I.P.O.N was forced to change its statutes after 2012, succumbing to Russian government actions and becoming subjugated to the Russian state and its economic interests in the Arctic.[37] Indigenous rights champion, Pavel Sulyandziga, was pushed out as a R.A.I.P.O.N candidate due to the new statutes. Sulyandizga unfairly lost to Ledkov, a member of Vladimir Putin's United Russia Party.[38]

Russia's true policy towards the Russian Saami is not to empower them, but is likely one of containment to prevent Saami political self-determination and to combat perceived Western intelligence exploitation of the Saami.[39] Russia's superficial advocacy for Saami cultural heritage may be assessed based on Russia's denial of funding for the preservation of the Saami language. Russian Saami on the Kola peninsula have been losing their language, and the younger Saami generations have learned Russian as their main language. Lack of political power and the loss of cultural heritage may cause the Russian Saami to become absorbed into Russia while being falsely represented by state-linked individuals who may falsely portray the relation between the Kola Saami and the Russian government.

The mechanics of false representation may be seen analogously through Russia's deception against Finland in the nuclear power industry. Russia utilized a Croatian front company to satisfy non-Russian ownership requirements for the Hanhikivi nuclear power plant in Finland,[40] which is scheduled to be built through a Finland-Russia venture, Fennovoima, utilizing Russia's state-owned company, Rosatom, as the supplier. The simulation of non-governmental appearances, while dissimulating the fact that the Russian government is behind the façade, is comparable to Russia's actions against the Russian Saami, though the deceit is much more overt in the actions against the Russian Saami.

Russia may influence trans-national Saami organizations through Russian state-linked individuals who have hijacked and controlled the Russian Saami. While the Saami are represented through R.A.I.P.O.N and are observers in the Nordic Council, they are also linked through the Arctic Council, of which Russia is a member state.[41] It is possible that Nordic Saami may be influenced by R.A.I.P.O.N through its international exchange and education programs. Exchange and education programs under Russian state influence may propagate humanitarian narratives that encourage political opposition against Nordic industrialization and militarization in the north.

In contrast to Russia's governmental control of the Russian Saami, the Finnish Saami do not appear to be infiltrated by the Finnish government. However, this may change in the future, and concerns have been raised over non-Saami infiltration into Finnish Saami politics.[42] Legislative action on Saami Parliament has been halted in the past,[43] due to contentions over the legal definition of a "Lapp" being too broad, and allowing non-Saami Finns residing in Lapland to become voting members of the Saami Parliament. It is unclear whether a recent proposal to revise the Act on the Sami

Parliament[44] will fix this problem in favor of the ethnic Saami, or continue to allow non-Saami Finns to influence Saami politics. The latter outcome could benefit the Finnish government as it could influence Saami politics internally through state sympathizers.

Another channel for Finnish control of the Finnish Saami may be through mission creep within the climate change agenda. Militarized exploitation of the climate change narrative may co-opt the Saami as a pretext for the securitization of Arctic interests. The Finnish government has linked the Lapland Saami to the climate change narrative,[45] and the Finnish Institute of International Affairs has previously suggested that climate securitization could be presented as humanitarianism.[46] The first "Arctic Resilience" forum in Finland was held recently in the fall of 2018, and involved the Finnish Ministry of Foreign Affairs in discussions about climate change.[47] This involvement is consistent with the issue of climate change treated as a security issue by the Finnish Ministry of Defense.[48]

Despite Finland and Russia's similarities in political oppression against the Saami, some of the methods employed reflect fundamental differences. The undemocratic nature of Putin's kleptocracy allows it to exercise more authoritarian approaches. State interference, corruption, infiltration, and control of Saami leadership is a top-down approach, while exploiting and manipulating Saami voting rights to create state-favorable outcomes is a bottom-up approach. Mission creep that seeks to manipulate the Saami into accepting governmental "protection" and cooperation against climate change is also a bottom-up approach. However, deceptive domestic influence operation utilized towards accomplishing foreign policy agendas will raise questions.

While the Saami are integral human factors to consider in any Arctic ambition, the Finnish Saami are likely more exploitable than the Russian Saami. The Russian Saami are losing their culture and more accepting of the political control against them than the Finnish Saami. Accelerated assimilation into Russia and lack of genuine political representation will increasingly allow the Russian government to hijack the Saami identity and exploit it. While superficially treated better than the Finnish Saami, the Russian Saami have fewer rights and are likely to suffer retaliation for political opposition under a kleptocratic regime.

Targeted with the proxied approach, the Finnish Saami may be vulnerable to Russian influence operations. According to a N.A.T.O publication, "Influencing public opinion in Finland and in many other countries is difficult, not least for historical reasons. Exerting influence may be easier when carried out indirectly and aimed at smaller target groups."[49] Given the small size of the Finnish Saami community, its marginalization, its historical and ongoing grievances against the Finnish government, and Finnish sensitivities towards overt Russian influence operations, the indirect approach may be the most likely route for Russia.

Given Russia's proven ability to leverage internet trolls, bot nets, and the media to influence perceptions, it is possible that Saami grievances and rights may be exploited, amplified, and weaponized against the Finnish government to prevent or delay further Western industrialization and militarization of Finland's northern area. Co-option and amplification may also be indirectly achieved through left-wing trans-national and international activist organizations, which may be influenced by Kremlin-linked political scientist, Aleksandr Dugin, whose political theory utilizes the co-option and exploitation of various ideological factions for strategic Russian interests.

In 2017, Aleksandr Dugin was hosted as a guest speaker in Helsinki by Johan Backman, a Kremlin foreign policy supporter who opposes N.A.T.O and the European Union. Backman is currently a Finnish candidate for Lapland's parliament. Given the sensitive political situation of northern Finland, Backman may serve as an enabler of Russia's political warfare against Finland.

Aleksandr Dugin's involvement with Backman is troubling, given Dugin's history of involvement with Russian influence operations. Dugin was banned by the U.S. Government in 2015 due to his involvement with separatists in the Ukraine crisis.[50] Dugin has also been involved with suspected Russian influence operations in Macedonia.[51] Dugin's 2017 involvement with Backman in Finland was likely an attempt at continuing political influence operations; the two have a history of attempting to foster Finland-Russia ties in 2014.[52]

However, due to Backman's exposure, it is questionable whether Backman could be overtly leveraged to exploit the Finnish Saami. While preventing or delaying Western industrialization and militarization of northern Finland are objectives that would benefit the Finnish Saami as well as the Kremlin, indirect Russian influence operations do not need to have the Finnish Saami take pro-Russia positions, or have Backman politically involved within Finnish Saami politics.

The Finnish Saami themselves may not seek or accept Backman's involvement, as political involvement with Backman may raise suspicions and further weaken the Finnish Saami's position against the Finnish government. Considering this, indirect Russian influence may be conducted through third parties, and only need to encourage Finnish Saami opposition to the Finnish government's actions in northern Finland.

The Finnish Saami may unwittingly be influenced by Russian influence operations that are discrete and proxied, e.g. through left-wing activist organizations, humanitarian organizations, etc. However, despite common objectives that logically benefit both the Finnish Saami and the Kremlin, the fact that the Finnish Saami oppose the Finnish government's actions against them does not necessarily imply that the Finnish Saami are agents of influence for Russia.

Given the subtle nature of indirect influence operations, even if the Finnish Saami become corrupted by the Russians, the Finnish Saami may not announce any overt intention or strategy to oppose the Finnish government in a manner that displays pro-Russia sentiments, and the Russians may not announce any intention or strategy to influence the Finnish Saami against the Finnish government. Therefore, predictive analysis and threat analysis may not utilize concrete language or solely rely on empirical, overt evidence of corruption as standards.

5 CONCLUSION

Finnish Lapland may become the future target of Kremlin influence operations. Lapland's Saami inhabitants have already displayed indicators of escalation in their opposition against the Finnish government's encroachment, and hold serious grievances against the Finnish government. The humanitarian issues of the Finnish Saami may be indirectly exploited by Russia to prevent or delay Western militarization and industrialization of Lapland. Such actions would benefit Russia and the Finnish Saami.

Johan Backman's political ambitions in Lapland, his history of overt pro-Kremlin actions, and his historical involvement with Aleksandr Dugin, are indicators of potential political influence operations in Lapland that will favor Kremlin foreign policy. While no definitive inferences may be drawn regarding the potential for collusion between Backman and the Finnish Saami, it is likely that attempts to co-opt or exploit the Finnish Saami will be indirect and discrete, and may not require Backman's involvement within Finnish Saami politics.

---

[i] The Security Strategy for Society, The Security Committee, Yhteiskunnan Turvallisuus, web. <https://turvallisuuskomitea.fi/wp-content/uploads/2018/04/YTS_2017_english.pdf>

[ii] Charly Salonius-Pasternak, An Effective Antidote: The Four Components That Make Finland Resilient to Hybrid Campaigns, Finnish Institute of International Affairs, web. <http://www.css.ethz.ch/content/dam/ethz/special-interest/gess/cis/center-for-securities-studies/resources/docs/FIIA-An%20Effective%20Antidote,%20The%20Four%20Components%20that%20Make%20Finland%20More%20Resilient%20to%20Hybrid%20Campaigns.pdf>

[iii] C.I.A World Factbook, Central Intelligence Agency, web. <https://arcticreview.no/index.php/arctic/article/view/729/2319>

[iv] Action Plan for the Update of the Arctic Strategy, Prime Minister's Office, Finland, web. < https://vnk.fi/documents/10616/3474615/EN_Arktisen+strategian+toimenpidesuunnitelma/0a755d6e-4b36-4533-a93b-9a430d08a29e/EN_Arktisen+strategian+toimenpidesuunnitelma.pdf>

[v] Christina Allard, The Rationale for the Duty to Consult Indigenous Peoples: Comparative Reflections from Nordic and Canadian Legal Contexts, Arctic Review on Law and Politics, web. < https://arcticreview.no/index.php/arctic/article/view/729/2319>

[vi] Report on the human rights situation of the Sami people in the Sapmi region, A/HRC/33/42/Add.3, United Nations General Assembly, web. < http://unsr.vtaulicorpuz.org/site/index.php/documents/country-reports/155-report-sapmi-2016>

[vii] Rene Nyberg, Hybrid Operations and the Importance of Resilience: Lessons from Recent Finnish History, Carnegie Endowment for International Peace, web. < http://carnegieendowment.org/2018/02/08/hybrid-operations-and-importance-of-resilience-lessons-from-recent-finnish-history-pub-75490>

[viii] REFORMI, web. <https://reformime.wordpress.com/lappi/>

ix Official Biography, Johan Backman, web. <http://johanbackman.ru/official-biography>

x Ibid.

xi Alexander Dugin in Helsinki, Geopoliical.ru, web. < https://www.geopolitica.ru/en/article/alexander-dugin-helsinki>

xii Alexander Dugin esitelmoi Helsingissa 11.4, Johan Backmanin blogi, web. < https://kohudosentti.blogspot.com/2017/04/alexander-dugin-esitelmoi-helsingissa.html>

xiii Cultural Diversity in Finland, FENNIA, web. <http://www.helsinki.fi/maantiede/geofi/fennia/demo/pages/raento.htm>

xiv Minister of Justice Defends Status of Russian Speakers Against Russian Speakers, UUTISET, web. <https://yle.fi/uutiset/osasto/news/minister_of_justice_defends_status_of_swedish_speakers_against_russian_speakers/6732037>

15 Emily J. Gertz, Indigenous People Are Fighting Finland's Plan to Log Ancient Forests, Take Part, web. <http://www.takepart.com/article/2016/03/24/finland-old-growth-arctic-boreal-forest-reindeer-sami-indigenous-land/>

16 Emily J. Gertz, Proposed Arctic Railway Would Cut Through Lapland Reindeer Habitat, High North News, web. <http://www.highnorthnews.com/proposed-arctic-railway-would-cut-through-lapland-reindeer-habitat/>

17 Lana Vidmar, The Sami and the Changing Arctic, Univerza V Ljubljani, web. <http://dk.fdv.uni-lj.si/magistrska/pdfs/mag_vidmar-lana.pdf>

18 Where the Truth Lies: Finland's New Attempts at Sami Reconciliation, News Now Finland, web. <http://newsnowfinland.fi/news-now-original/where-the-truth-lies-finlands-new-attempts-at-sami-reconciliation>

19 Sami Activists Occupy Island in Protest at Tenojoki Fishing Rules, YLE News, web. <https://yle.fi/uutiset/osasto/news/sami_activists_occupy_island_in_protest_at_tenojoki_fishing_rules/9717663>

[20] Cree Leaders Join Anti-Railway Demonstrations in Finland, APT National News, web. <http://aptnnews.ca/2018/09/06/cree-leaders-join-anti-railway-demonstrations-in-finland/>

[21] Finland to Deploy Quick Response Units Along Russian Border, Defense News, web. <https://www.defensenews.com/land/2015/07/18/finland-to-deploy-quick-response-units-along-russian-border/>

[22] Ibid.

[23] Finland's Ever-Evolving Defense Doctrine, Military Periscope, web. < https://apps.militaryperiscope.com/SpecialReports/ShowReport.aspx?report=9 27 >

[24] Winter Training Exercise of Utti Jaeger Regiment in Lapland, Finnish Defense Forces, web. < https://puolustusvoimat.fi/en/article/-/asset_publisher/1950813/utin-jaakarirykmentin-talviharjoitus-lapissa >

[25] Norway's Secret Surveillance of Russian Politics for the NSA, Dagbladet, web. <https://www.dagbladet.no/nyheter/norways-secret-surveillance-of-russian-politics-for-the-nsa/61923431>

[26] Reid Standish, How a Norwegian Retiree Got Caught Up in a Spy Scandal, The Atlantic, web. <https://www.theatlantic.com/international/archive/2018/05/how-a-norwegian-retiree-got-caught-up-in-a-spy-scandal/560657/>

[27] Nina Berglund, Spying Recruiters Target Kirkenes, Views and News from Norway, web. <http://www.newsinenglish.no/2018/04/29/spying-recruiters-target-kirkenes/>

[28] Russia Brands Arctic Indigenous Organization As "Foreign Agent," Eye on the Arctic, web. <http://www.rcinet.ca/eye-on-the-arctic/2015/09/25/russia-brands-arctic-indigenous-organization-as-foreign-agent/>

[29] Andrej Kotljarchuk, Kola Sami in the Stalinist Terror: A Quantitative Analysis, Journal of Northern Studies, Vol. 6, No. 2, web. <http://www.diva-portal.org/smash/get/diva2:606912/FULLTEXT01.pdf>

[30] Russian Security Council, "Principles of the State Policy of the Russian

Federation in the Arctic Until 2020 and Future Perspectives," Russian Arctic Strategy, web. <http://www.scrf.gov.ru/documents/98.html>

[31] Andrey Dalinov, Elections or Farce?, Arctic Consult, web. <https://arcticconsulteng.wordpress.com/2018/07/01/2018-06-andrey-danilov-elections-or-farce-some-thoughts-about-elections-at-the-association-of-the-kola-sami/>

[32] Ibid.

[33] Ministry of Domestic Policy and Mass Communications of the Murmansk Region, Murmansk Regional Government, web. <https://eng.gov-murman.ru/authorities/ministries/ministry_of_inte/>

[34] The New President of the Kola Saami, Hand of Moscow, web. <http://handofmoscow.com/2018/06/28/the-new-president-of-the-kola-saami/>

[35] Andrey Dalinov, Elections or Farce?, Arctic Consult, web. <https://arcticconsulteng.wordpress.com/2018/07/01/2018-06-andrey-danilov-elections-or-farce-some-thoughts-about-elections-at-the-association-of-the-kola-sami/>

[36] Russia: Activists Prevented from Traveling to UN Meeting, Human Rights Watch, web. < https://www.hrw.org/news/2014/09/25/russia-activists-prevented-traveling-un-meeting>

[37] Mikkel Berg-Nordlie, Two Centuries of Russian Sami Policy: Arrangements for Autonomy and Participation Seen in Light of Imperial, Soviet and Federal Indigenous Minority Policy 1822-2014, Acta Borealia, Vol. 32, Issue 1, web. <https://blogg.hioa.no/sapmirussia/files/2015/10/1443789454.pdf>

[38] Ibid.

[39] 9 августа во всём мире отмечают День коренных народов мира. Но в Мурманске запланированные торжества саамов прошли с громким скандалом!, Horizontal Russia 7x7, web. <https://7x7-journal.ru/item/20144>

[40] Ibid.

41 Arctic Council, web. <https://arctic-council.org/index.php/en/about-us/member-states/russian-federation>

42 Report on the Current Situation of the Sami People in Finland, YLE News, web.
<https://yle.fi/uutiset/osasto/sapmi/report_on_the_current_situation_of_the_sami_people_in_finland/8877972>

43 Christina Allard, The Rationale for the Duty to Consult Indigenous Peoples: Comparative Reflections from Nordic and Canadian Legal Contexts, Arctic Review, S.1, V.9, web. <
https://arcticreview.no/index.php/arctic/article/view/729/2316 >

44 Yle Sapmi, Act on Sami Parliament Up For Reform in Finland, The Barents Obvserver, web. < https://thebarentsobserver.com/en/2017/12/act-sami-parliament-reform-finland>

45 Climate Change and the Finnish Sami, Climate Guide, web. <https://ilmasto-opas.fi/en/ilmastonmuutos/vaikutukset/-/artikkeli/98d25017-430a-405b-80f3-ddefcc534d75/saamelaiset.html>

46 Emma Hakala, Strategy of Necessity for Finland?, FIIA Briefing Paper 209, The Finnish Institute of International Affairs, web.
<https://storage.googleapis.com/upi-live/2017/04/bp209_climate_security.pdf>

47 Finding Ways for the Environment to Cope with Climate Change, Arctic Finland, web. <https://www.arcticfinland.fi/news/Finding-ways-for-the-environment-to-cope-with-climate-change/39969/b41ffca6-67d4-46b3-8ad1-e1cf1d6bc1e5>

48 Jaana Sorvali, Links Between CCVI and National Risk Assessments in Finland, National Resources Institute Finland, web.
<https://forum.eionet.europa.eu/nrc-climate-change-adaptation/library/workshops-meetings/2018-expert-meeting-national-climate-chnage-vulnerability-and-risk-assessments/meeting-documents/presentations/11_group_2.a_cca_drr_finland/download/en/1/11_Group_2.A_CCA_DRR_Finland.pdf>

---

[49] Katri Pynnoniemi and Sinikukkua Saari, Hybrid Influences – Lessons from Finland, NATO Review, NATO, web. <https://www.nato.int/docu/review/2017/also-in-2017/lessons-from-finland-influence-russia-policty-security/EN/index.htm>

[50] Ukraine Crisis: US Sanctions Target Russia Idologue, BBC, web. < https://www.bbc.com/news/world-us-canada-31838096>

[51] Fatima Tlis, Disinfo Analysis: Macedonia – To Be or Not to Be… Russia's Satellite, Polygraph.info, web. < https://www.polygraph.info/a/macedonia-russia-meddling-disinformation/29278930.html>

[52] Anna Nemtsova, Finland and the Bear, Foreign Policy, web. < https://foreignpolicy.com/2018/07/31/finland-and-the-bear-russia-putin-trump-finns-helsinki/>